9<u>11</u>
9PROMISE

Promises, Prayers and Inspiring Quotations for
Life, Liberty and True Happiness in Crisis or Calm

Daniel Williams

CREATION
HOUSE
PRESS

911 Promise by Daniel Williams
Published by Creation House Press
A part of Strang Communications Company
600 Rinehart Road
Lake Mary, Florida 32746
www.creationhouse.com

All scriptures quoted, unless otherwise noted, are
from the Holy Bible, New International Version.
Copyright © 1973, 1978, 1984, International Bible
Society. Used by Permission.

Cover design by Debbie Lewis

Library of Congress Control Number: 2002105473
International Standard Book Number:
0-88419-927-4

02 03 04 05   8 7 6 5 4 3 2 1
Printed in the United States of America

This book is dedicated to
my wife Sharon,
to our dear friends
Angelo and Cindy D'Amico,
to Angelo's mother, Marie D'Amico,
whose comments inspired the
direction of this book,
and to all who helped
with research and input.

Acknowledgments

Special acknowledgment is given to Penny Scott and Robyn Rhoads for their research and editorial contributions.

CONTENTS

PREFACE

Our nation has been awak-
ened by the worst attack on
U.S. soil in our history. Where
were you on 9/11 when the news of
events began to spread? First, an
airliner hit the North Tower of the
World Trade Center...

   ...then the South Tower was
      hit
   ...then the Pentagon
   ...then the crash in
      Pennsylvania
   ...then the collapses.

As I hurriedly drove toward my
office, I wondered what it all
meant as my mind reflected back
to several defining moments that I

had passed through as a citizen of this nation. Scenes from my past flashed into my mind: My great-grandmother nervously rocking, wringing her hands and wondering aloud, "Who could do such a thing?" as televised reports poured out of Dallas informing us that our president had been mortally wounded. Other memories raced through my thoughts: the Cuban Missile Crisis, the Vietnam War, the Challenger Explosion, Oklahoma City, Columbine.

Then I was at the office gathering our staff together to strategize our response when the people began to come. There were one or two at first, mostly teenagers and college students. More trickled in that day, and they kept coming into the night as we prayed. The next day was the same, and the next...

What will become of us as a result of this terrorist strike? More importantly, what can we do in response? Will military might or political cunning be able to deliver us from future assaults? Is there more that we can do?

There is much more.

A slogan was popularized in one of Ford Motor Company's early safe-driving campaigns, which said, "Look up and get the big picture." This campaign reminded drivers to check their rearview mirrors, glance from side to side and look farther out in front of them for dangers that might be lurking ahead. This slogan could serve as a good model for each of us as individuals and for all of us as a nation. We need to ask ourselves, What have we done in the past that could have contributed to this situation? What is our current situation? What is ahead? Are we seeing the big picture?

Many have weighed in on what might have precipitated this horror. Others have discussed and are discussing our response. This book will focus on what is ahead. I will leave the secular discussions to the geopolitical powers who must focus on our human response. May they have God's wisdom.

In the Bible, we learn that "He [God] has given us his very great and precious promises" (2 Pet. 1:4). My goal for this book is to discover what God has promised for those upon whom His favor dwells and how we may call upon His promises in prayer.

The genesis of this book was a casual dinner conversation with a close friend. He shared with me how his mother had directed him to several passages of scripture that contained great promises of protection and blessing. All of the scriptures happened to have "911" as reference numbers. Inspired by my friend's remarks, I began looking up other 911 passages. Every day across America, people in emergency situations of life call 911. However, it is important that we know whom to call. Let us never neglect to call upon God's Word for help.

With this in mind, I present this book of 911 promises, prayers and special quotations.

—DANIEL WILLIAMS

Our scientific power has
outrun our spiritual power.
We have guided missiles and
misguided men.
—Dr. Martin Luther King Jr.

We do not need more material development, we need more spiritual development. We do not need more intellectual power, we need more moral power. We do not need more knowledge, we need more character. We do not need more government, we need more culture. We do not need more law, we need more religion. We do not need more of the things that are seen, we need more of the things that are unseen.

—PRESIDENT CALVIN COOLIDGE

ONE

A Promise Of
PROTECTION

911 Promise

I establish my covenant with
you: Never again will all life be
cut off by the waters of a flood;
never again will there be a flood
to destroy the earth.
—Genesis 9:11

This 911 passage comes from the story of Noah and the ark. Most of us are familiar with what happened during the flood, but many of us are not as clear about what brought it about in the first place. We read in Genesis 6:5–6, "The LORD saw how great man's wickedness on the earth had become, and that every inclination of the thoughts of his heart was only evil all the time. The LORD was grieved that he had made man on the earth, and his heart was filled with pain." Have you ever regretted having known someone you loved? Most of us have felt the sting of disappointment that love can bring. It is difficult to grasp that God also feels the pain of broken relationships. All too often when things become this painful we just walk away. Instead of walking away, God looked for a reason to remain committed to mankind, and He found Noah to "stand in the gap."

In Ezekiel 22:30 we read: "I looked for a man among them who would build up the wall and stand before me in the gap on behalf of the land so I would not have to destroy it, but I found none." The intention of God's heart is evident here. He wanted a person through whom He could establish an agreement, a covenant. It was not God's desire to destroy mankind or the earth, which He created in love.

> THOSE WHO KNOW LITTLE OF GOD'S LOVE AND SUPREMACY OVER HIS OWN CREATION LIVE IN CONSTANT FEAR. HOW SAD. THEY DO NOT UNDERSTAND THAT THERE ARE HIGHER LAWS THAN OUR OWN AT WORK. GOD'S WILL AND SOVEREIGNTY WILL PREVAIL.

God is committed to the human race. Simply stated, He loves us, and the very nature of that love is the establishment of lasting bonds. Therefore, mankind was created to exist in a continuous, unabridged and infinite relationship with God—a relationship maintained through an everlasting covenant. Rather than looking for ways to destroy us or separate Himself from us, God continually seeks deeper connection.

This understanding of the nature of God's relationship to us is vital to our faith. The moment we comprehend that He is forever seeking to establish us in a covenant relationship with Him, our faith rises to a new level of effectiveness. Instead of prayers filled with doubt and fear about the future, we can pray with full assurance of His love and care for us. "'For I know the plans I have for you,' declares the LORD, 'plans to prosper you and not to harm you, plans to give you hope and a future'" (Jer. 2<u>9:11</u>).

Our Genesis <u>9:11</u> passage makes it clear that the entire earth will not be destroyed without God's approval. Doomsayers and fear-mongers are always present. They say that the earth will be destroyed by nuclear war. Or, they threaten that the planet will be destroyed by industrial pollution. Others warn that life on earth will end by a giant meteor. Although these are legitimate issues worthy of our consideration and appropriate responses, God made this planet and its people for His own pur-poses. The Bible says, "The heavens are yours, and yours also the earth; you founded the world and all that is in it" (Ps. 8<u>9:11</u>).

We do not have to live our lives in constant fear of destruction. God reserves the rights to the earth and its inhabitants for Himself. Understanding this gives me a sense of calm and peace about the future. The same God who created the world loved it so much that He sent His Son to redeem it. This world will not end until it is time to replace it with something far better. What a deal!

Sadly, those who know little of God's love and supremacy over His own creation live in constant fear. They do not understand that there are higher laws than our own at work. God's will and sovereignty will prevail.

Some have seized upon 9/11 as a reason to believe that our nation is doomed and our future ruined. Fear makes small problems seem much larger. The effects of 9/11 are by no means small. Yet this event, too, shall pass. It has changed us as a nation, but I believe for the better. Once again the truth of God's Word is demonstrated to us: "And we know that in all things God works for the good of those who love him, who have been called according to his purpose" (Rom. 8:28).

We must view the events of 9/11, and for that matter any other circumstance of life, from a spiritual perspective. Circumstances vary, but God's promises are unchangeable. "So we fix our eyes not on what is seen, but what is unseen. For what is seen is temporary, but what is unseen is eternal" (2 Cor. 4:18). We must learn to rely upon spiritual strength. Indescribable peace is available to the person who acknowledges and trusts God. The Bible says, "He who dwells in the shelter of the Most High will rest in the shadow of the Almighty" (Ps. 91:1). As we move beyond September 11, 2001 or any other life crisis, we can do so with confidence in God's ability to protect us and preserve us for the future He has planned for us.

"For through me your days will be many, and years will be added to your life" (Prov. 9:11).

"Leave your orphans; I will protect their lives. Your widows too can trust in me" (Jer. 49:11).

911 PRAYER OF PROTECTION

Father in heaven, You are my shield and strong tower. Thank You for Your unfailing love and covenant that will endure beyond the existence of this earth. I put my whole trust in You and know that You have plans for my prosperity, health, significance and long life. I pray for my family that each of us will walk in safety, wholeness and obedience to You. Thank You that no weapon formed against us will prosper and that every tongue that rises up against us will be condemned. I know that You have given Your angels charge over us and that You have promised to be a hedge around us. Surely no enemy can pass through without Your notice. You turn what the enemy means for evil into good.

I pray for The United States of America, which was founded on the premise that You are our Creator and that You oversee the affairs of men. Forgive us for our ignorance of Your will; cover us with Your mercy and cleanse us in the precious blood of the Lamb. Cause our leaders, military personnel and citizenry to dwell in safety. May you cause the very elements of creation to stand with us in our battles as You did for Moses, Joshua and Deborah. Draw each citizen to salvation in the name of Jesus Christ, and confound the forces of evil where they seek to destroy our land. You are our God, our Father and our source of life, love and safety. May Your name be exalted above every enemy in this land, and may our highest destiny be fulfilled in each of our lives and in our nation. In the matchless name of Jesus Christ our Savior, amen.

This is the real task before us: to
reassert our commitment as a
nation to a law higher than our
own, to renew our spiritual
strength. Only by building a wall
of such spiritual resolve can we,
as a free people, hope to protect
our own heritage and make it
someday the birthright
of all men.
—PRESIDENT RONALD REAGAN

Our constitution was made for a moral and religious people. It is wholly inadequate to the government of any other.

—JOHN ADAMS

TWO

A Promise of
GUIDANCE

---

911 PROMISE:
At the end of the forty days
and forty nights, the LORD gave
me the two stone tablets, the
tablets of the covenant.
—DEUTERONOMY 9:11

The entire nation of Israel had lived as slaves for hundreds of years. They were Hebrew by birth, but deeply steeped in the culture and values of Egypt. Once delivered from slavery, God began to lead them into both outward and inward freedom. What must it have been like to go from constant control by their Egyptian masters to complete freedom?

Imagine an entire nation freed from slavery at once. There was no system of government, no laws, no order. They needed guidelines for their newfound freedom. Every nation must have a moral guidance system upon which it depends for ethics and conduct. God gave them guidance by giving them a covenant anchored by the Ten Commandments. These Commandments contain spiritual principles for life.

Principles are self-evident truths that are generally recognized in all human cultures. Honesty, for instance, is universally accepted as being preferred over dishonesty. We sometimes choose dishonesty over truth for convenience, gain or even safety. Nevertheless, lying makes us feel dirty and inwardly violated. When we compromise our principles and lie, eventually truth becomes blurred and our world degenerates into a swirl of half-truths and falsehoods. Honesty often hurts at the outset, but it brings peace and a sense of wholeness in time. Honesty feels good because it is right.

> EVERY NATION MUST HAVE A MORAL GUIDANCE SYSTEM UPON WHICH IT DEPENDS FOR ITS ETHICS AND CONDUCT.

These principles for living are not solely religious, although most enduring religions embrace them as essential. Nor are these principles simply social mores based on culture. Societies and cultures come and go, but the basic principles of fairness, integrity, hard work and all such principles transcend cultural changes.

Principles need little explanation. They simply make sense. It is as if the human spirit is predisposed to hold dear these basic convictions. We were designed, it seems, to understand and value these creeds of life. Whether we openly resist them or simply neglect them, these intrinsic principles gnaw at our insides, demanding our consideration of their virtue.

This does not mean that we do not have to work to maintain principle-centered living. In fact, it is a daily battle to keep from being swept away into the abyss of cultural degeneration. People can seem to descend to the lowest common denominator except in rare times of crisis. This leads to downward spiraling values. As individuals, it is our responsibility to stand against this cultural tendency to lower our values by living our own lives according to godly principles.

The need to take a stand for principle-centered living is reinforced in my own life by the knowledge that my family is deeply affected by the principles I exhibit. I am personally grateful for the Bible and for my relationship with the risen Christ. Though personal principles are indeed self-evident, the simple clarity of God's Word and the effect of His holy presence bring needed power and grace to my pursuit of principle-centered living. For our own sake, for our families' sake and for the sake of our nation, we must make it a priority to rediscover the principles found in the Bible and live by them.

A nation is no stronger than the moral character of its people. We each play an important role in the future of our land. Our individual commitment to live for God and follow His ways is vital. This personal commitment changes families. Families change communities. Communities change counties, counties change states, and states change the nation. How can our nation be changed? It must be changed one individual at a time. It makes little sense to hope for significant change in our nation if we cannot commit to personal change.

This nation is uniquely blessed to

have been established with a strong biblical foundation. When one visits the Capitol building in Washington, D.C., the scriptural underpinnings of our nation's religious foundation are easily seen. At every level our nation must turn to the God of Scripture. Individual Christians, churches, educational institutions and government leaders must rely again on the moral foundation upon which this nation was built. We do not necessarily need a Christian government. Too many historical and modern examples exist in which divine and human institutions were blended and resulted in tyrannical governments. We do, however, need a government that practices the Christian values upon which it was founded.

Historical revisionists would have us believe that our nation's founders were generally secularists. Even a superficial study of history dispels such a notion. Some were humanists, and some who professed Christianity were imperfect in their private lives. But such examples are few, and they are greatly overshadowed by the many Christian founders who practiced genuine faith during the founding of this nation. A huge body of conspicuous evidence exists to support this fact. Therefore, we must emphatically declare and insist that our hope is based upon biblical values.

Those who envisioned the laws of this nation were, for the most part, practicing Christians whose consciences and values laid a foundation for the laws that we inherited. Our American democracy needs its Christian underpinnings, and we cannot function devoid of Christian values and divine guidance. Only God's Word can lead us out of the errors of mankind by paving a highway of truth through the mountains of confusion.

"I will turn all my mountains into roads, and my highways will be raised up" (Isa. 49:11).

911 PRAYER OF GUIDANCE

Majestic Father, thank You for not leaving us without guidance. Your Word gives us direction and clarity for living in the protection of Your covenant. Help us to understand Your ways, and give us grace to walk in them.

Guide me now in all areas of my life, and open the eyes of my understanding so that I will perceive Your direction. Remove from me every way that is displeasing to You, and write Your laws on my heart. Direct my family in the perfect paths prepared for them, and cause them to walk in the good works created for them from the foundation of the world. Draw each person in this nation to seek Your kingdom and righteousness and to discard his or her own ways. Deliver us from all prejudice, and help us to respond to every human need with compassion. Help our governmental leaders, our clergy, our educators, our news media and our entertainers to awaken to the spiritual principles found in the Bible. Speak to us and empower us to follow You.

By Your Holy Spirit, enlighten us to recognize the covenant You have with our leaders and with us. Purify our hearts and minds so that we will always be able to avail ourselves of Your divine guidance. In Jesus name, amen.

It cannot be emphasized too strongly or too often that this great nation was founded not by religionists, but by Christians, not on religion, but on the gospel of Jesus Christ. For this very reason peoples of other faith have been afforded asylum, prosperity and freedom of worship here.
—PATRICK HENRY

I shall allow no man to belittle my soul, by making me hate him.

—Booker T. Washington

THREE

A PROMISE OF
DELIVERANCE

911 PROMISE:
You divided the sea before
them, so that they passed
through it on dry ground, but
you hurled their pursuers into
the depths, like a stone
into mighty waters.
—NEHEMIAH 9:11

G od made a way for His people to be delivered from those who hated and persecuted them. When all seems hopeless, God makes a way. As a nation recently freed from hundreds of years of slavery, Israel was ill equipped to defend itself. The Israelites were servants, not soldiers. They had no training for battle. Their defenselessness actually worked to their benefit, for no other avenue for deliverance was available except God. He was their only source.

There is a spiritual principle here; "When I am weak, then am I strong" (2 Cor. 12:10). How bizarre to the human mind, yet simple to the spiritual mind; He does more with less. This is based on a simple premise: the less He has to work with the more He does. I refer to this process as "God's Divine Reduction Plan."

In the story of Gideon, we find that God's concern was quite the opposite of Gideon's. Gideon had done all that he could to gather as many soldiers as possible. The enemy he was facing was well equipped and had a huge number of battle-hardened warriors. But God's response to Gideon's effort surprised everyone. God reduced Gideon's army from 32,000 to 10,000 to 300. "The Lord said to Gideon, 'You have too many men for me to deliver Midian into their hands. In order that Israel may not boast against me that her own strength has saved her" (Judg. 7:2). God did deliver Gideon's enemies into his hands with just 300 men. When we are weak, He is strong in us and for us. In such circumstances, we witness God's Divine Reduction Plan at work. God does more with less.

Need more evidence? Consider how Jesus fed the multitudes. This actually occurred twice with similar circumstances but different numbers. The differing results of the two separate incidences are very telling. In one of the events there were five thousand hungry people (Matt. 14:16–21). The disciples of Jesus produced five loaves of bread and two fish and presented them to Jesus. He blessed the bread and fish and proceeded to feed all five thousand with the broken pieces. After everyone had their fill, twelve baskets of leftovers were collected. In other words, five loaves of bread, plus two fish, minus five thousand people equals twelve baskets left over: 5+2-5,000=12.

In the second incident (Matt. 15:33–38), there were fewer people, four thousand, and there was more food: seven loaves of bread and a few small fish. After everyone had their fill, only seven baskets were left over. In other words, seven loaves of bread, plus three or more fish, minus four thousand people equals seven baskets left over: 7+3-4,000=7. This vividly illustrates how God does more with less and less with more.

> WHEN WE ARE IN RIGHT RELATIONSHIP TO GOD, WE FALL UNDER HIS PROTECTION, OVERSIGHT AND DELIVERANCE.

The result of this principle is that since God reduces our involvement to bring forth the greater results, we are freed from the responsibility to enact wrath upon our enemies. God will judge those who act hatefully. He will often use human governments as a part of His judgment process. Yet we, as individual Christians, are not permitted to hate or enact our own personal wrath, no matter how angry we may feel. We read in Matthew 5:43–44, "You have heard that it was said, 'Love your neighbor and hate your enemy.' But I tell you: Love your enemies and pray for those who persecute you, that you may be sons of your Father in heaven."

These are difficult passages to receive. They force us to acknowledge that God alone is capable of fair and absolute judgment. Human revenge accomplishes nothing. When we are in right relationship to God we come under His protection, oversight and deliverance. And our enemies fall under His judgment. "Only do not rebel against the LORD. And do not be afraid of the people of the land, because we will swallow them up. Their protection is gone, but the LORD is with us. Do not be afraid of them" (Num. 14:9). So what is the Christian response when our nation is attacked?

- **To those who are our enemy.** Romans 12:18–21 "If it is possible, as far as it depends on you, live at peace with everyone. Do not take revenge, my friends, but leave room for God's wrath, for it is written: 'It is mine to avenge; I will repay,' says the Lord. On the contrary: "If your enemy is hungry,

41

feed him; if he is thirsty, give him something to drink. In doing this, you will heap burning coals on his head." Do not be overcome by evil, but overcome evil with good."

- **To Satan and the forces of evil.** James 4:7 "Submit yourselves, then, to God. Resist the devil, and he will flee from you."

- **To those who are in government.** 1 Timothy 2:1–4 "I urge, then, first of all, that requests, prayers, intercession and thanksgiving be made for everyone—for kings and all those in authority, that we may live peaceful and quiet lives in all godliness and holiness. This is good, and pleases God our Savior, who wants all men to be saved and to come to a knowledge of the truth."

- **To those who are called upon to sacrifice their own safety in the defense of their nation.** John 15:13 says, "Greater love has no one than this, that he lay down his life for his friends."

911 PROMISES

A man's wisdom gives him patience; it is to his glory to overlook an offense.

—PROV. 1<u>9:11</u>

The LORD gives strength to his people; the LORD blesses his people with peace.

—PS. 2<u>9:11</u>

911 PRAYER OF DELIVERANCE

Oh God of power and might, we echo the words of our Lord Jesus as we petition: "Deliver us from evil."

King David cried out to You and You delivered him from all his enemies, both within and without. We, too, have many who rise up against us and say that there is no help for us in God. Lord, help us to see that You fight for those who trust in You.

By Your great name, crush every trap into which I, my family and my people have fallen. Cause us to stand in Your strength alone. Direct our paths that we might not stumble and fall into danger and sin. Nations are against us and seek to condemn and destroy us. Empower us with Your strength and love so that our enemies will be defeated. Help us to forgive and bless our enemies with Your love and truth. Enable us to live at peace with all men as much as is possible, and cause Your love, which never fails, to be our greatest motivation.

Thank You, Lord, for all who in brave dedication to this nation heed the call to serve in harm's way. Preserve every life from intentional or accidental harm. May every person in this land be delivered from those things that are not of You, and may the plans of the prince of darkness be thwarted and his power annulled. Open to us a path of deliverance. In the name above every name, we pray, amen.

A Promise of Deliverance

We are not retreating; we are advancing in another direction.
—GENERAL DOUGLAS MACARTHUR

The spirit of man is more important than mere physical strength and the spiritual fiber of a nation than its wealth.

—PRESIDENT DWIGHT D. EISENHOWER

FOUR

A Promise of
PROCLAMATION

---

911 Promise:

Sing praises to the Lord,
enthroned in Zion; proclaim
among the nations what
he has done.
—Psalm 9:11

Catastrophes have a way of being so all consuming that it becomes difficult to remember what preceded the moment of crisis and what things might lie ahead. When really bad things happen it is natural to focus on the circumstances. The worse the situation, the more absorbing it is, until we find that we just can't think of anything else.

The beginning point for overcoming tragedy is to pursue God.

As we behold Him, the circumstances of life begin to come into proper perspective. What is temporary becomes swallowed up by the eternal. Paul E. Billheimer, the well-loved writer and pastor, has said: "The worship and praise of God demands a shift of center from self to God. One cannot praise without relinquishing occupation with self." As we enter into the true worship of God, the hurts and fears we feel begin to slip away. Praise validates the sovereignty of God in our souls. As we enthrone Him in our situations through praise and recognition of His awesomeness, we will gain strength to move forward.

David was a worshiper long before he became king of Israel.

His words capture the spirit of his relationship with God: "Shout for joy to the LORD, all the earth. Worship the LORD with gladness; come before him with joyful songs. Know that the LORD is God. It is he who made us, and we are his; we are his people, the sheep of his pasture. Enter his gates with thanksgiving and his courts with praise; give thanks to him and praise his name. For the LORD is good and his love endures forever; his faithfulness continues through all generations" (Ps. 100:1–5).

SOON, THE EFFECT OF PRAISE ON OUR SOUL PROVOKES US TO PROCLAIM HIS GREATNESS TO OTHERS.

Notice how praise took David from an acknowledgment of God as Creator and Lord to an understanding of Him as a shepherd who could meet every need. From here David progressed to having fresh insight into the very nature of God's love and faithfulness, which transcends the temporary and goes from generation to generation. Praise has the same effect for us.

The effect of praise upon our souls provokes us to proclaim God's greatness to others. The testimony of God goes forth as a witness to His goodness and majestic power toward all who trust in Him. Our voice of praise becomes a voice of proclamation, heralding God's majestic power, which encircles the earth.

Our greatest influence as a nation will not be established on the battlefields or in the boardrooms of the world, but rather in the hearts of men and women. To the extent that we effectively declare His glory among the peoples of the earth will we see nations change for the better.

This 911 promise reminds us that God is still on His throne. It also gives us direction for the next emergency of life. When in peril we must praise Him! When devastated we must praise Him! When suffering the pain of loss we must praise Him! In the Book of Acts, we find the apostle Paul in horrible circumstances. "About midnight Paul and Silas were praying and singing hymns to God, and the other prisoners were listening to them. Suddenly there was such a violent earthquake that the foundations of the prison were shaken. At once all the prison doors flew open and everybody's chains came loose" (Acts 16:25–26).

Paul and Silas had discovered the power of praise. They had mastered a secret for success in life that carried them through. "But we have this treasure in jars of clay to show that this all-surpassing power is from God and not from us. We are hard pressed on every side, but not crushed; perplexed, but not in despair; persecuted, but not abandoned; struck down, but not destroyed" (2 Cor. 4:7–9).

Sir William Temple, the esteemed seventeenth century diplomat and author, declared: "Worship is the nourishment of the mind upon God's truth. Worship is the quickening of the conscience by God's holiness. Worship is the cleansing of the imagination by God's beauty. Worship is the response of my life to God's plan for my life."

Our individual futures and well-being, as well as that of our nation, depend upon our true praise and worship of God and His sovereignty.

911 PRAYER OF PRAISE

Blessed be God, ruler of the universe. I exalt and glorify Your holy name. Truly there is none like You. You are the source of life, beauty, goodness and love. By your wisdom the worlds were framed and everything is upheld by the power of Your Word. I worship and glorify You. May my life, my family, my community and my nation become a fountain of praise and gratitude to You.

May Your name and deeds be continually on our lips while Your love fills our hearts. You have delivered us, You have rebuked the devourer for us and You have increased our prosperity.

58

A Promise of Proclamation

You have given our people great understanding and have helped us to build a nation of freedom, invention, commerce, health and strength. You have caused us to dwell in peace within our borders and have used us to be a blessing to millions around the world.

In the advancement of Your kingdom, You have blessed us with great churches, godly examples, airwaves filled with the light and life, an abundance of teaching and worldwide significance. Even when times are difficult, You cause all things to work together for the good of those who love You. Thank You, most holy Father for the greatest gift of all, Your Son who died that we might live with You forever. Blessed be Your holy name forevermore! Amen.

We have this day restored the
Sovereign to whom all men
ought to be obedient. He reigns
in heaven and from the rising
to the setting of the sun.
Let His kingdom come.
—SAMUEL ADAMS

As God gives us to see the right, let us strive on to finish the work we are in. To bind up the nation's wounds, to care for him who shall have borne the battle, and for his widow and his orphan—to do all which may achieve and cherish a just and lasting peace among ourselves and with all nations.

—President Abraham Lincoln

FIVE

PROMISE OF

RESTORATION

---

911 PROMISE:

In that day I will restore David's
fallen tent. I will repair its
broken places, restore its ruins,
and build it as it used to be.
—AMOS 9:11

The wind was tearing away the roof of our neighbor's house. A tall pine tree was slowly bowing toward the ground, its roots protruding from the earth. The rain was hitting our windows like machine gun fire. It was 1964 and Hurricane Dora was ripping away our city. It would take weeks to assess the true extent of Dora's destructive force. The shoreline was the hardest hit. Blocks of homes and businesses...gone. Buildings that were left standing looked as if they had been bombed.

How does a community recover from such devastation? Compared to other disasters in other times and places, ours was modest. But it was our disaster. The loss was personal.

What do you do when everything is gone?

Our city recovered. New homes replaced those that had been completely destroyed. Damaged homes were repaired and gleamed like new. The restoration process provided an opportunity to replace outdated fixtures and systems. New wiring, new plumbing, fresh paint, updated insulation—the restored homes were actually better than before!

OUR RESTORATION PROCESS MUST BEGIN WITH PERSONAL RESTORATION TO THE PRINCIPLES OF GOD AND TRUST IN HIS ABILITY TO RESCUE, REFORM AND REDEEM.

In our Amos 9:11 passage, we are given hope for rebuilding every destructive situation of life. God proclaims "I will restore...I will repair." We can count on God's supernatural involvement and help; then again, we, too, have a part in the restoration process. Isaiah 58:12 declares: "Your people will rebuild the ancient ruins and will raise up the age-old foundations; you will be called Repairer of Broken Walls, Restorer of Streets with Dwellings." God's restoration requires partnership. He will most certainly do His part if we will do ours.

As a component of our rebuilding process, we should examine ourselves carefully. Not everything that has been destroyed should be replaced as it was. The ruined buildings in Manhattan and Washington, D.C., will be the easiest part of the 9/11 restoration process. The devastated lives and our national psyche will require a far more complicated process.

A falling away from God's principles often precedes the bad things that happen in life. The protection that a right relationship with Him affords us is sacrificed for our disobedience. Whereas God loves mankind, Satan hates us.

The devil will seize any opportunity to bring mayhem and destruction upon us very quickly. So often the evil that is wrought comes as human immorality. You know that Satan is at work and evil is present when one person takes advantage of another, one cultural group is prejudiced against another, economic oppression exists or anyone is intentionally subjugated for an immoral purpose.

I cannot recall another period in my lifetime when there has been so much open discussion of God, values and religion in general. We have a unique window of opportunity to identify and root out of our national culture those things that rob us of God's favor and protection.

As always, this process of change

must begin at the church's doorstep. "For it is time for judgment to begin with the family of God" (1 Pet. 4:17). Christians often complain about how laws and government have adversely affected our Christian values and practices. Nonetheless, we have a government and system of law that is "by the people." A nation is a collective of individuals. How we individually live our lives matters. If we abdicate our responsibility of upholding morality to others, then how can we legitimately complain about the results.

Every attitude and action within us that is contrary to true love for our fellowman must be exposed and replaced with godliness. Justice for all will come only when each individual determines to live a just life before God. Our restoration process must begin with our being personally restored to the principles of God, and we must choose to trust in His ability to rescue, reform and redeem.

911 PRAYER OF RESTORATION

Great Redeemer and Restorer, I have not walked in all Your ways and followed all Your precepts. There are areas in my life that have not been subject to Your direction. Because of this, I have suffered great loss and destruction. Please forgive me and enable me to submit to Your plan and discipline. Restore to me the joy of Your salvation and renew a right spirit within me.

Our fathers and our children have not kept Your Word as foremost in their lives and have forgotten many of the truths they have learned. Remind us of all that You have worked in us in the past, and enable us to walk in wisdom and obedience to You.

Our nation has sustained terrible attacks from both within and without our borders. Lives have been lost and families have been forever torn apart. You promised in Your Word to restore and repair our broken places and ruins, and I know that You will. Use me to be a repairer of broken walls and a restorer of streets with dwellings. Sweep away the wrong mindsets in our land, and replace them with the attitudes of Christ. Our country must serve You so that we can live in safety and peace. Draw us by Your Holy Spirit to Your Son, Jesus, and conform us completely to His image. In the perfect name of Jesus, amen.

Fondly we do hope, fervently
we do pray, that this mighty
scourge of war may speedily
pass away.
—PRESIDENT ABRAHAM LINCOLN

SIX

FINAL
WORDS

Perhaps you've begun to find some of your own powerful 911 promise passages before you've even completed your initial reading of this short volume. If so, that is precisely the point of this book.

In every situation of life, God's Word provides needed answers. Promises and guidance can be found on every page. The personal difficulties and life situations that you are currently facing or may someday have to face could make what happened on September 11, 2001, seem irrelevant to your own life. With God, there is no scale of importance when it comes to His love for the people He created in loving purpose and then redeemed for Himself at so great a cost.

He sees a sparrow that falls to the ground, and He sees nations in turmoil. He is a God who is never distracted by the least or the greatest. Your issues are never too large or too small to lay them at the Master's feet. Heaven is wide open to us and is not bankrupt; it cannot be overwhelmed and never loses its joy or peace. Studying the Bible, praying believing prayers and having humble hearts open to

us the windows of heaven for our
lives today.

> WITH GOD, THERE IS NO SCALE
> OF IMPORTANCE WHEN IT COMES
> TO HIS LOVE FOR THE PEOPLE HE
> CREATED IN LOVING PURPOSE AND
> THEN REDEEMED FOR HIMSELF AT
> SO GREAT A COST.

My hope is that you find solace
and inspiration in this book. But
my greater hope is that it may
point you toward that which will
give you a personal guidance
system for navigating through life:
God's wonderful Word.

I close with this final 911 passage:

> *"I saw heaven standing open
> and there before me was a*

white horse, whose rider is called Faithful and True. With justice He judges and makes war."

—Revelation <u>19:11</u>

To contact the author:

Write: DQuest Group
         39 South Roscoe Blvd.
         Ponte Vedra Beach, FL 32082

Phone: (904) 285-3308

Email: dquestgroup@yahoo.com